Traditional Hymn

Complements All Piano Methods

Table of Contents

Traditional Hymns Level 2 is designed for use with the second book of any piano method. Some methods may label their second book as *Book 2* (such as the *Hal Leonard Student Piano Library*), and others may label their second book as *Book 1*.

Concepts in *Level 2*:

Range	Symbols
	p, mp, mf, f, ♯, ♭, ♮, ⌒, *8va, ritard,* :‖
Rhythm	**Intervals**
4/4 time signature	2nd, 3rd, 4th and 5th
3/4 time signature	melodic and harmonic

ISBN 978-0-634-03678-1

HAL•LEONARD®
CORPORATION
7777 W. BLUEMOUND RD. P.O. BOX 13819 MILWAUKEE, WI 53213

Visit Hal Leonard Online at
www.halleonard.com

All Glory, Laud And Honor

Words by Theodulph of Orleans
Translated by John Mason Neale
Music by Melchior Teschner
Arranged by Fred Kern

in the Lord's name com - est, the King and Bless - ed One. All
we with all cre - a - tion in chor - us make re -

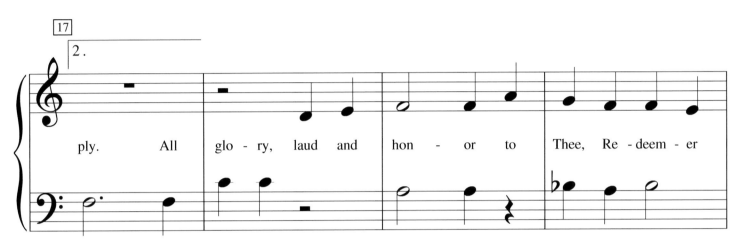

ply. All glo - ry, laud and hon - or to Thee, Re - deem - er

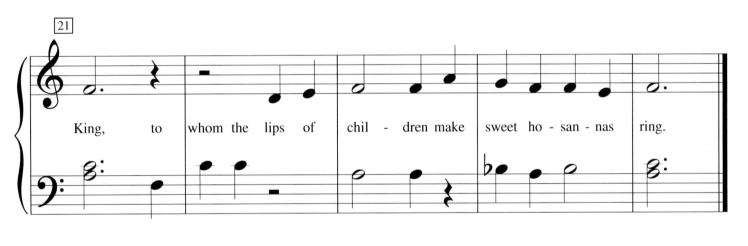

King, to whom the lips of chil - dren make sweet ho - san - nas ring.

Be Still, My Soul

Words by Katharina von Schlegel
Translated by Katharina von Schlegel
Music by Jean Sibelius
Arranged by Mona Rejino

With reverence (♩ = 88)

mp Be still, my soul; the Lord is on thy side. _____ Bear pa - tient - ly the cross of grief or pain. _____

_____ Leave to thy God to or - der and pro - vide; _____

Accompaniment (Student plays one octave higher than written.) 3/4 2

With reverence (♩ = 88)

p

mf

mp

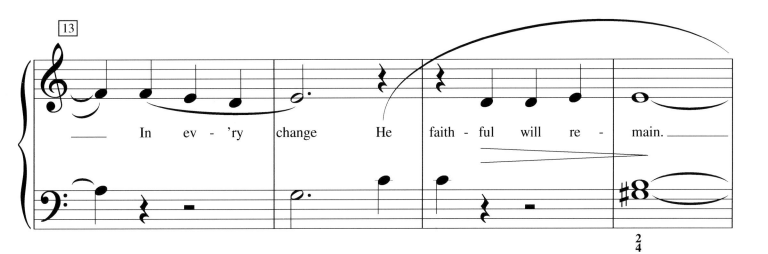

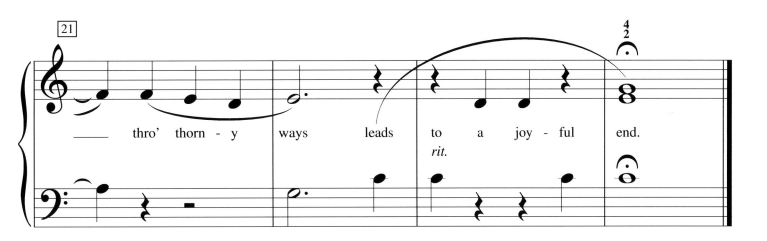

Come, Christians, Join To Sing

Words by Christian Henry Bateman
Traditional Spanish Melody
Arranged by Phillip Keveren

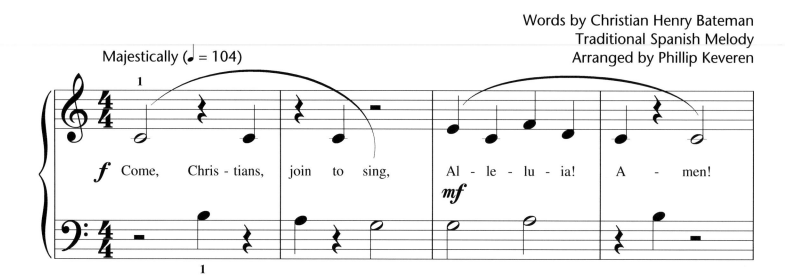

Accompaniment (Student plays one octave higher than written.)

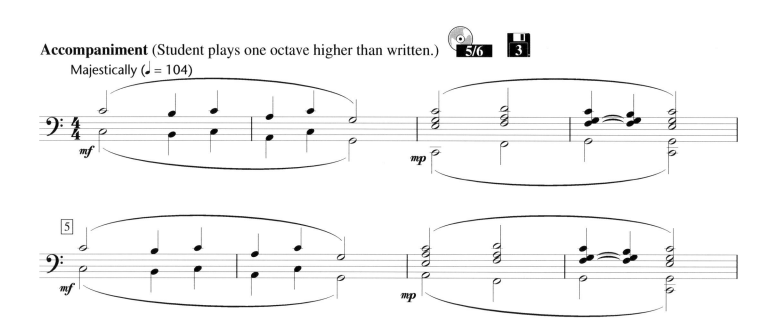

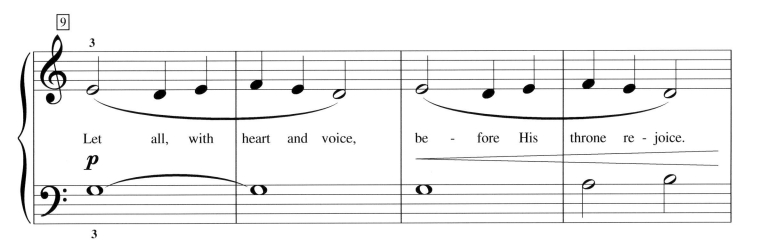

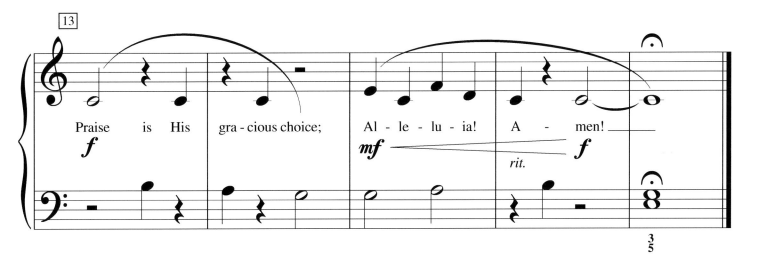

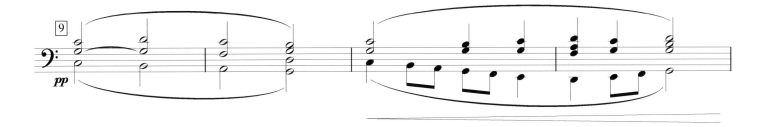

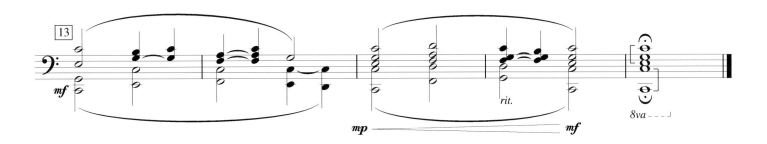

Down In My Heart

Traditional
Arranged by Phillip Keveren

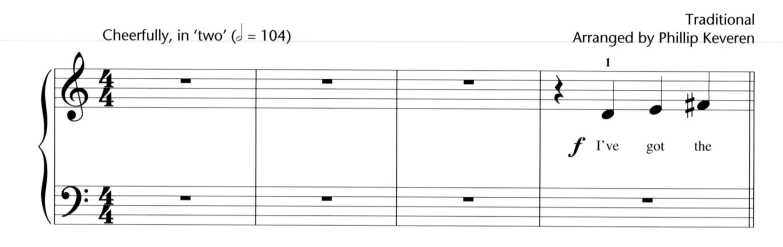

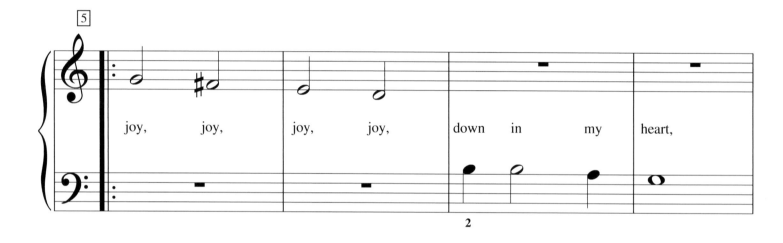

Accompaniment (Student plays one octave higher than written.)

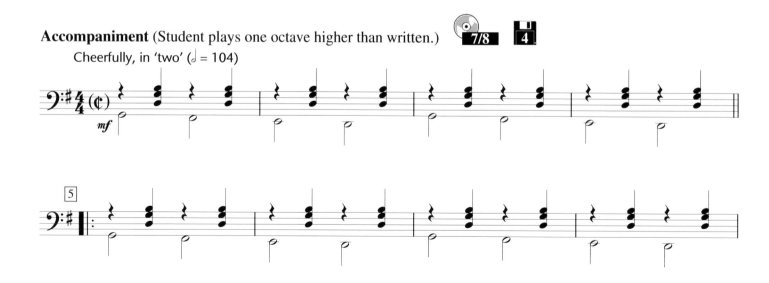

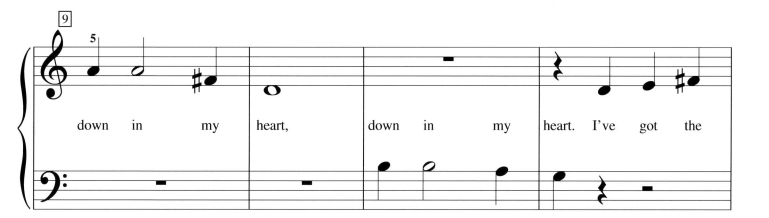

down in my heart, down in my heart. I've got the

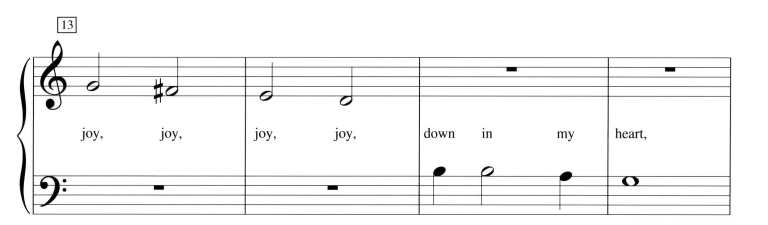

joy, joy, joy, joy, down in my heart,

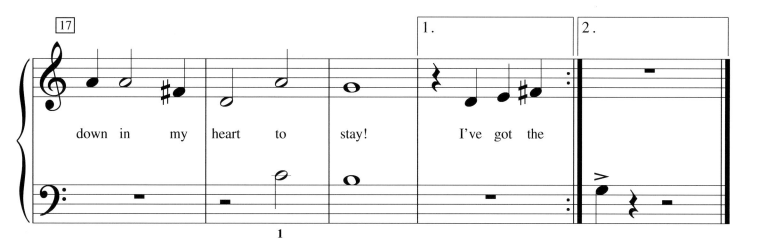

down in my heart to stay! I've got the

1

I Sing The Mighty Power Of God

Words by Isaac Watts
Traditional English Melody
Arranged by Mona Rejino

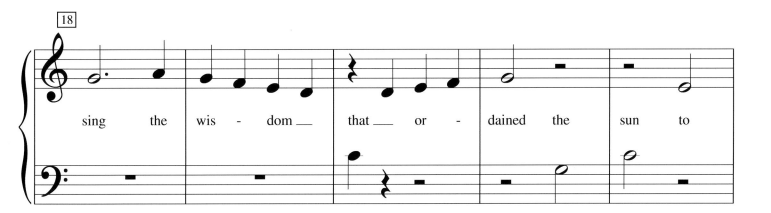

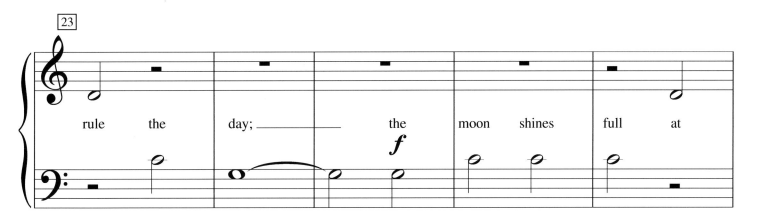

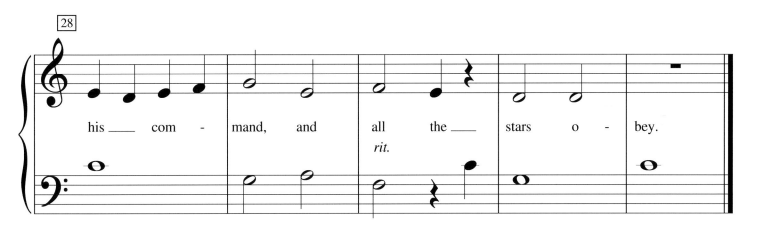

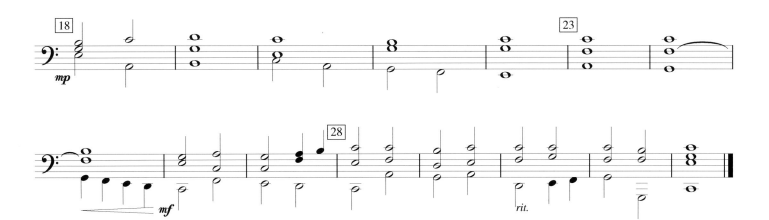

Joyful, Joyful, We Adore Thee

Words by Henry van Dyke
Music by Ludwig van Beethoven, melody from Ninth Symphony
Adapted by Edward Hodges
Arranged by Fred Kern

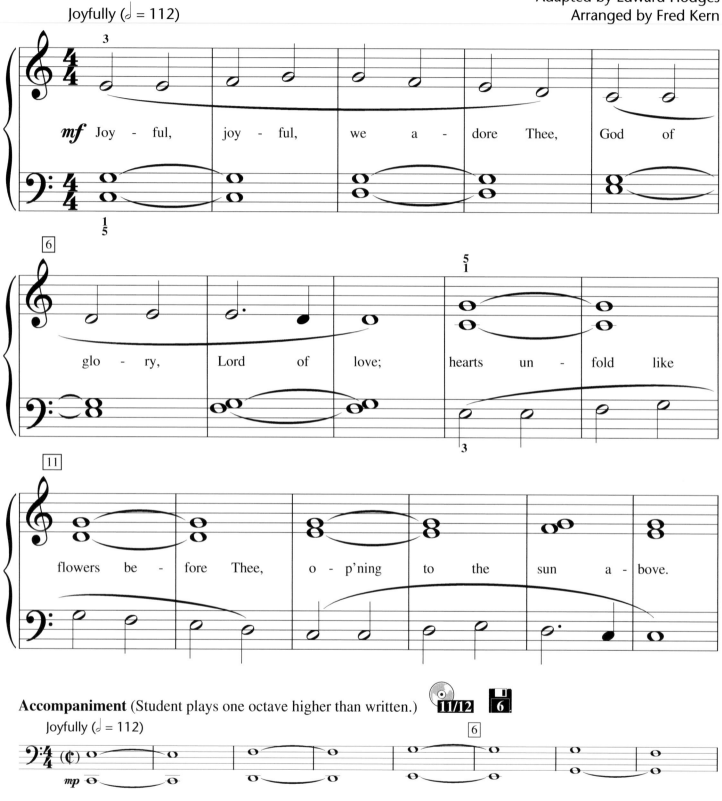

Accompaniment (Student plays one octave higher than written.)

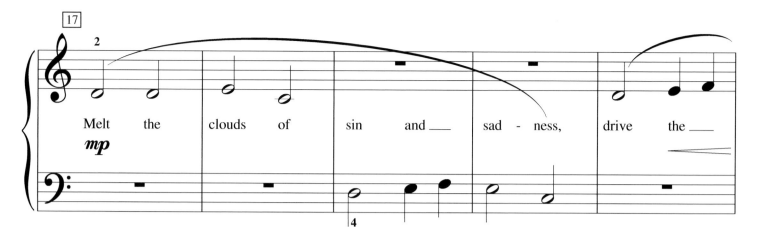

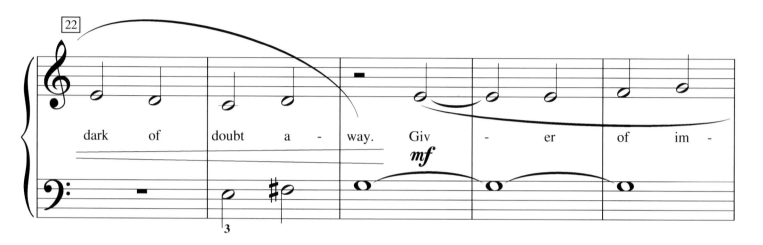

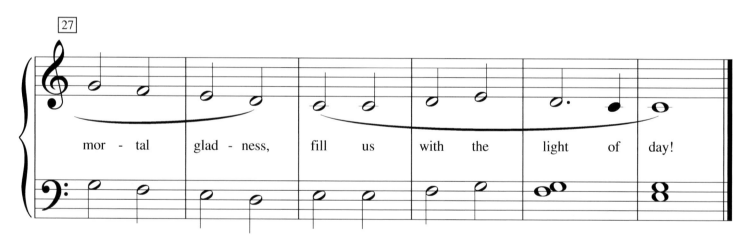

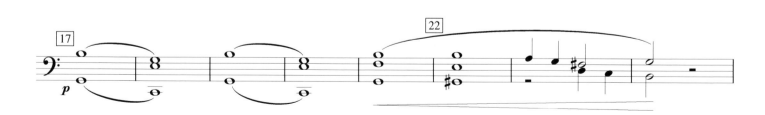

13

Now Thank We All Our God

German Words by Martin Rinkart
English Translation by Catherine Winkworth
Music by Johann Crüger
Arranged by Mona Rejino

from our moth-er's arms hath blessed us on our way with

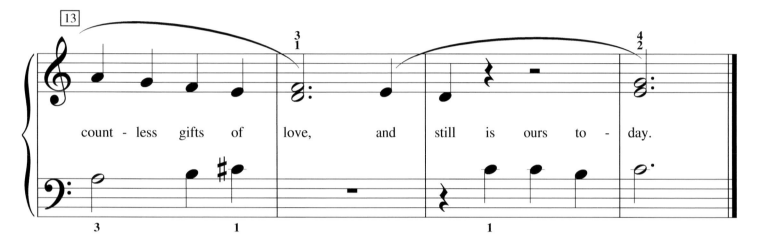

count - less gifts of love, and still is ours to - day.

15

O Worship The King

Words by Robert Grant
Music attributed to Johann Michael Haydn
Arranged by Phillip Keveren

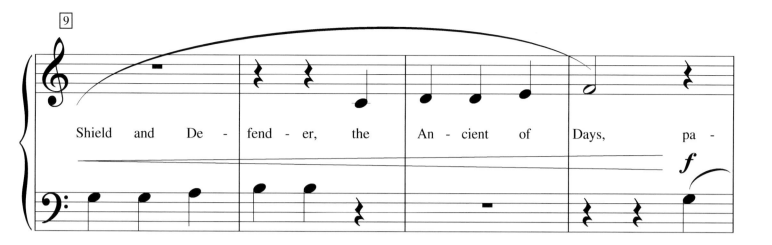

Praise Him, All Ye Little Children

Traditional Words
Music by Carey Bonner
Arranged by Fred Kern

With spirit, 'in two' (♩ = 92)

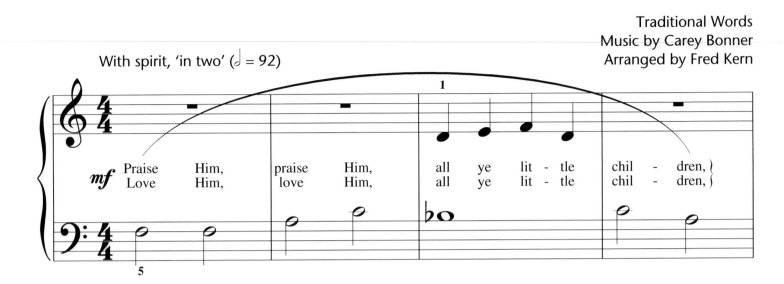

Praise Him, praise Him, all ye lit - tle chil - dren,
Love Him, love Him, all ye lit - tle chil - dren,

God is love, God is love.

Accompaniment (Student plays one octave higher than written.)

With spirit, 'in two' (♩ = 92)

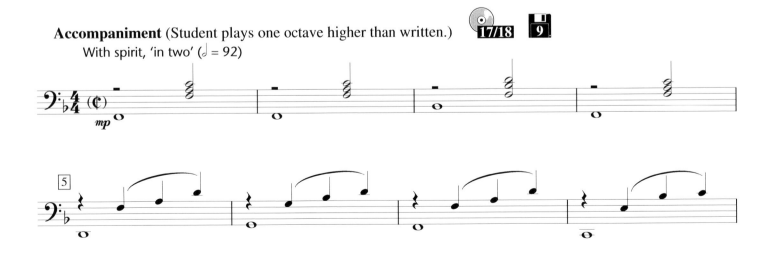

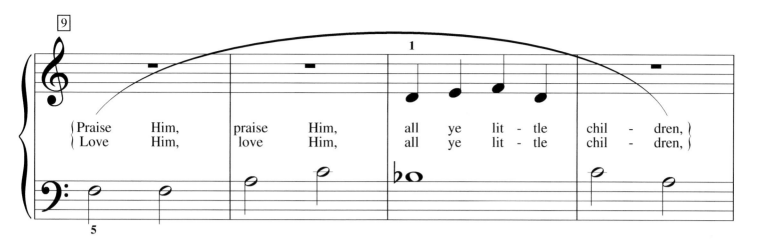

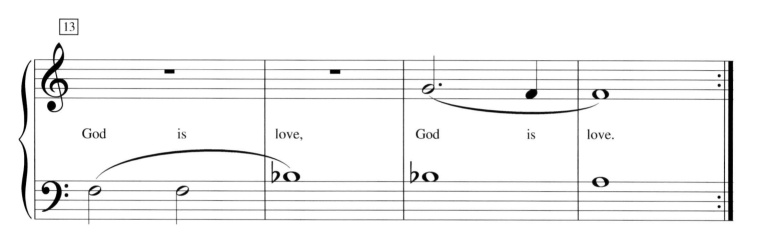

Sun Of My Soul

Words by John Keble
Music from Katholisches Gesangbuch
Arranged by Mona Rejino

Flowing (♩ = 96)

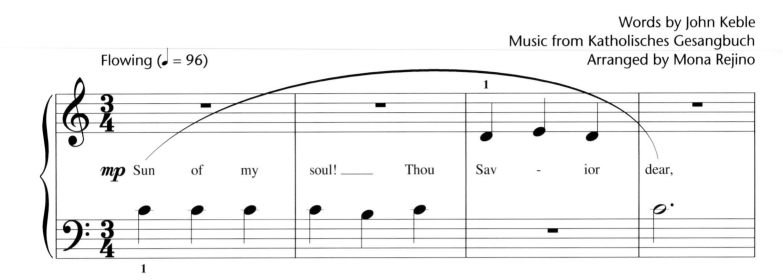

Sun of my soul! ___ Thou Sav - ior dear,

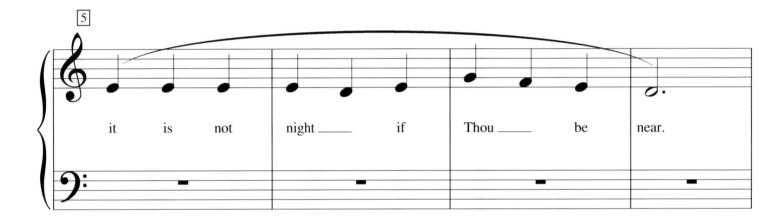

it is not night ___ if Thou ___ be near.

Accompaniment (Student plays one octave higher than written.) 19/20 10

Flowing (♩ = 96)

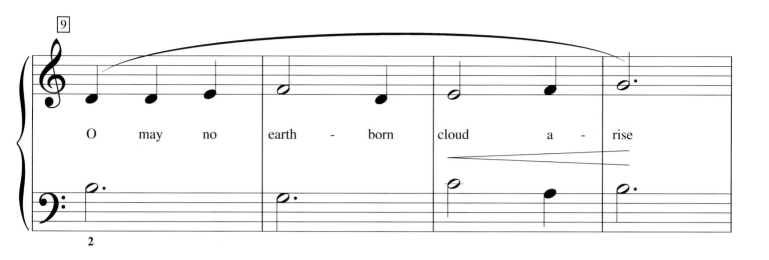

O may no earth- born cloud a - rise

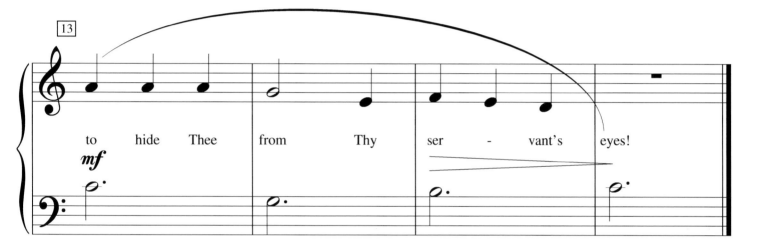

to hide Thee from Thy ser - vant's eyes!

mf

With pedal

mp

What A Friend We Have In Jesus

Words by Joseph M. Scriven
Music by Charles C. Converse
Arranged by Phillip Keveren

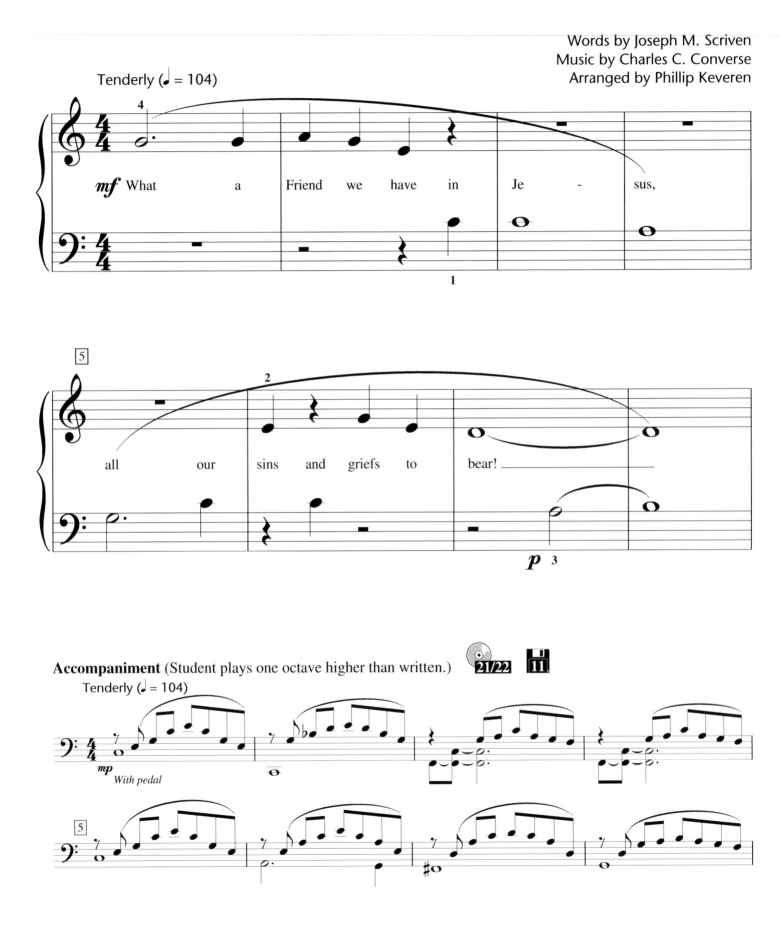

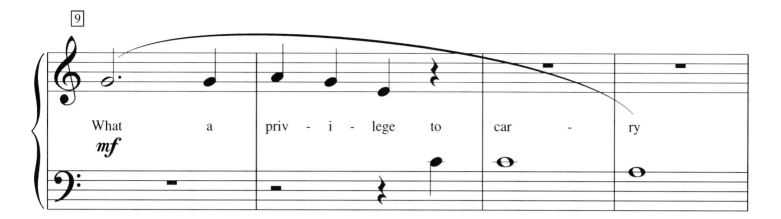

What a priv - i - lege to car - ry

mf

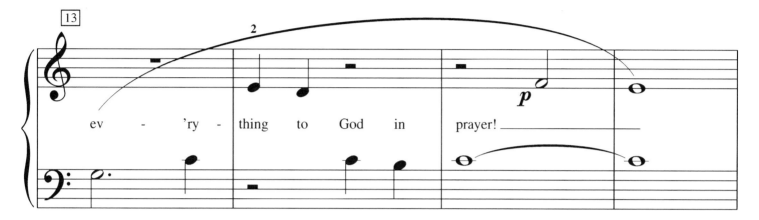

ev - 'ry - thing to God in prayer! _____

p

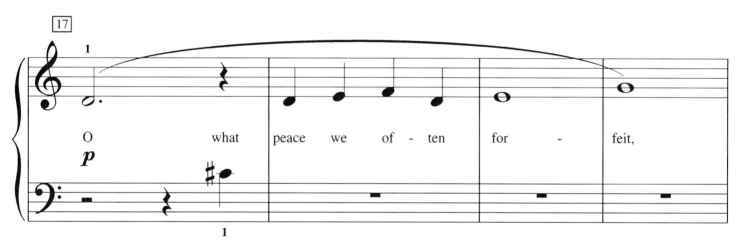

O what peace we of - ten for - feit,

p

pp

23

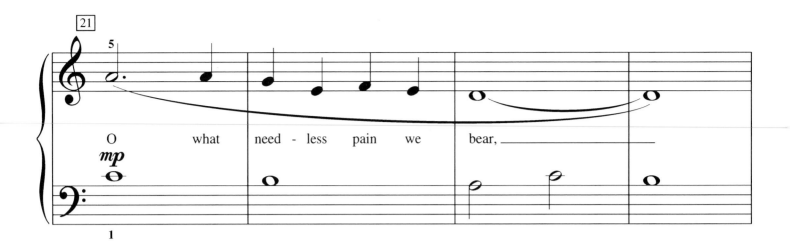

O   what   need - less   pain   we   bear,_____

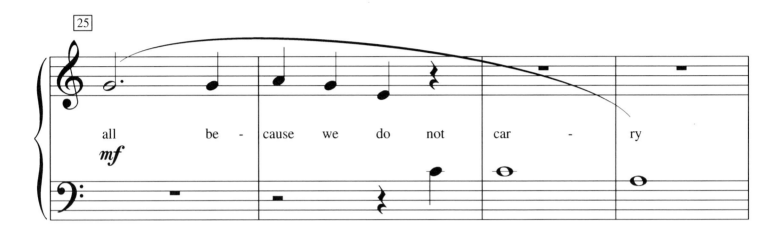

all   be -   cause   we   do   not   car -   ry

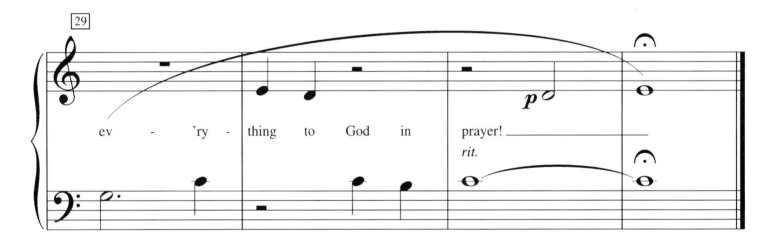

ev -   'ry -   thing   to   God   in   prayer!_____